HIT MOVIE SONGS
FOR BEGINNING PIANO SOLO

ISBN 978-1-5400-8900-7

Visit Hal Leonard Online at
www.halleonard.com

Contact us:
Hal Leonard
7777 West Bluemound Road
Milwaukee, WI 53213
Email: info@halleonard.com

In Europe, contact:
Hal Leonard Europe Limited
42 Wigmore Street
Marylebone, London, W1U 2RN
Email: info@halleonardeurope.com

In Australia, contact:
Hal Leonard Australia Pty. Ltd.
4 Lentara Court
Cheltenham, Victoria, 3192 Australia
Email: info@halleonard.com.au

CRAZY LITTLE THING CALLED LOVE

from the Motion Picture BOHEMIAN RHAPSODY

Words and Music by
FREDDIE MERCURY

Moderately fast Shuffle

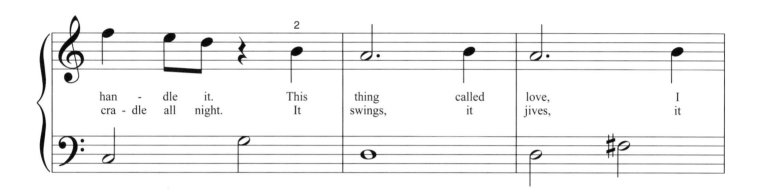

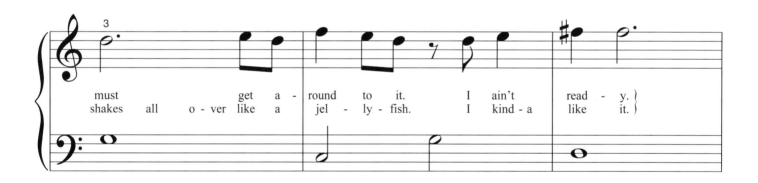

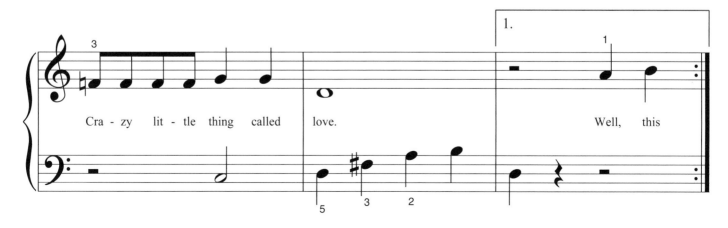

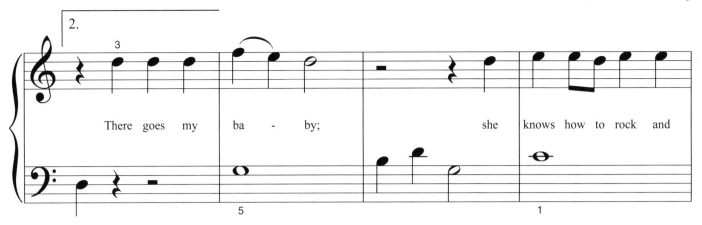

There goes my ba - by; she knows how to rock and

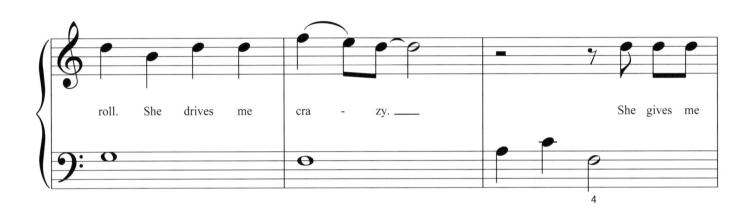

roll. She drives me cra - zy. ___ She gives me

hot and cold fe - ver. She leaves me in a cool, cool sweat.

I got - ta be cool, re -

lax,   get   hip,   get   on   my   tracks. Take a   back   seat,   hitch -

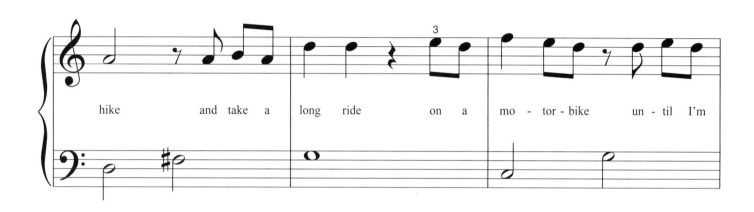

hike   and take a   long   ride   on   a   mo - tor - bike   un - til   I'm

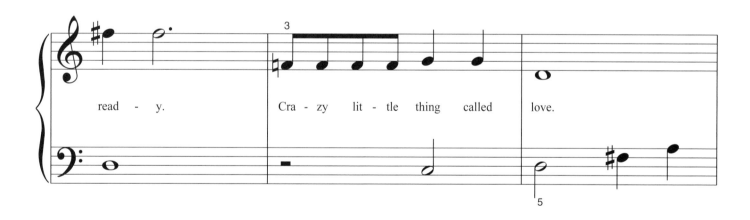

read - y.   Cra - zy   lit - tle   thing   called   love.

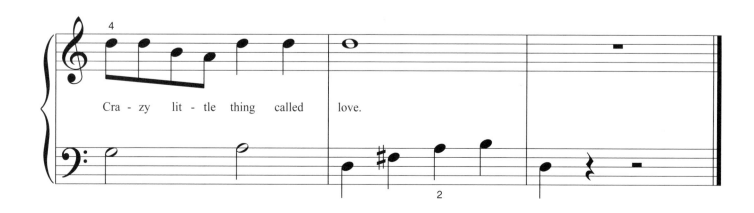

Cra - zy lit - tle thing called   love.

THE PLACE WHERE LOST THINGS GO

from MARY POPPINS RETURNS

Music by MARC SHAIMAN
Lyrics by SCOT WITTMAN
and MARC SHAIMAN

Gently, not slow

Do you ev-er lie a-wake at night, just be-tween the dark and the

morn-ing light, search-ing for the things you used to know,

look-ing for the place where the lost things go? Do you ev-er dream or

rem - i - nisce, won-d'ring where to find what you tru - ly miss?

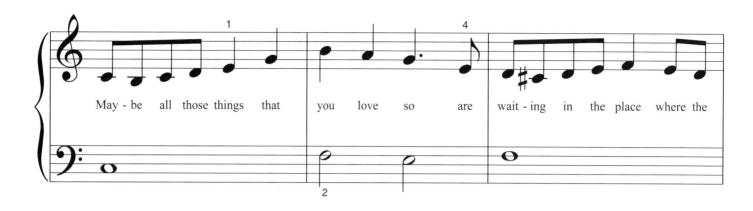

May - be all those things that you love so are wait - ing in the place where the

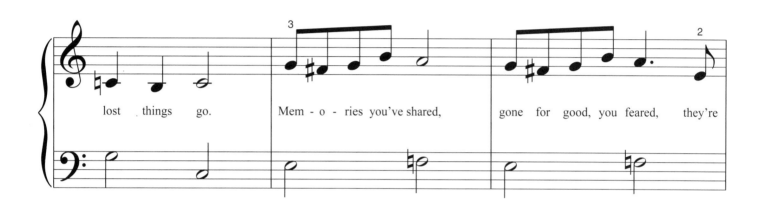

lost things go. Mem - o - ries you've shared, gone for good, you feared, they're

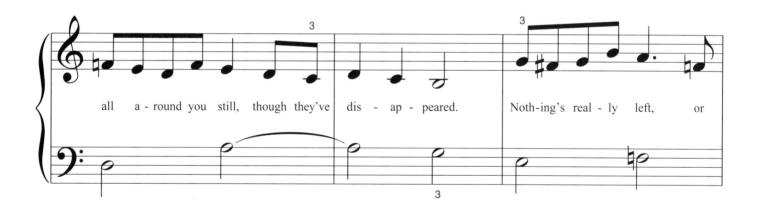

all a - round you still, though they've dis - ap - peared. Noth-ing's real - ly left, or

lost with - out a trace. Noth-ing's gone for - ev - er, on - ly out of place. So

may - be now the dish and my best spoon are play - ing hide and seek just be -

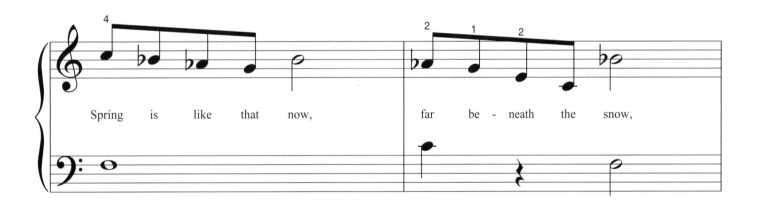

hind the moon, wait - ing there un - til it's time to show.

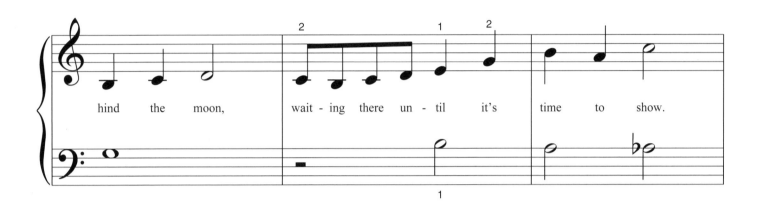

Spring is like that now, far be - neath the snow,

hid - ing in the place where the lost things go.

DOWNTON ABBEY

(Theme)

from the Motion Picture DOWNTON ABBEY

Music by JOHN LUNN

With motion

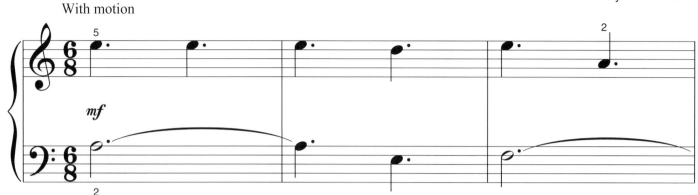

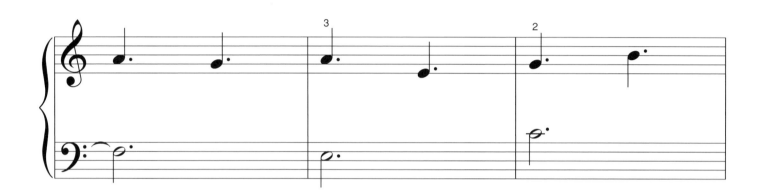

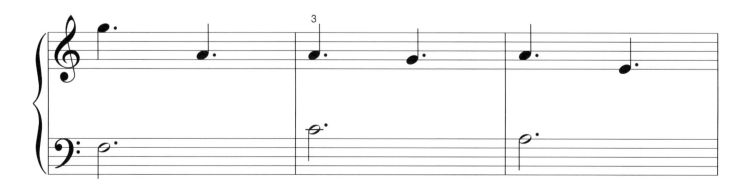

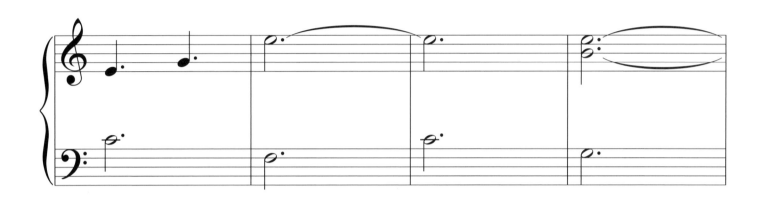

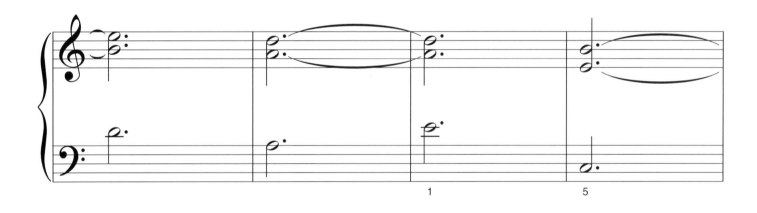

THE HIDDEN WORLD

from the Motion Picture HOW TO TRAIN YOUR DRAGON: THE HIDDEN WORLD

By JOHN POWELL

A MILLION DREAMS

from THE GREATEST SHOWMAN

Words and Music by BENJ PASEK
and JUSTIN PAUL

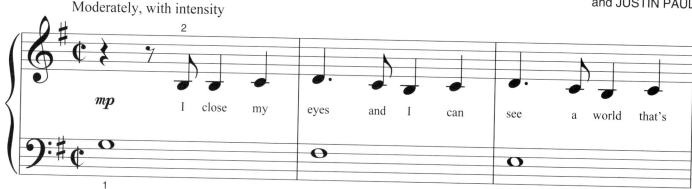

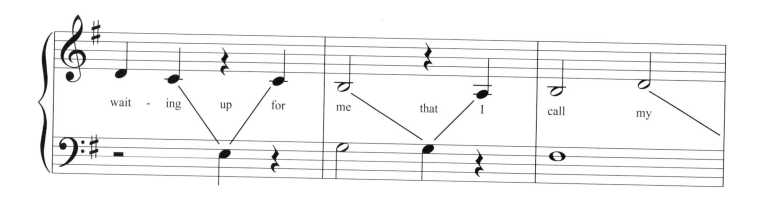

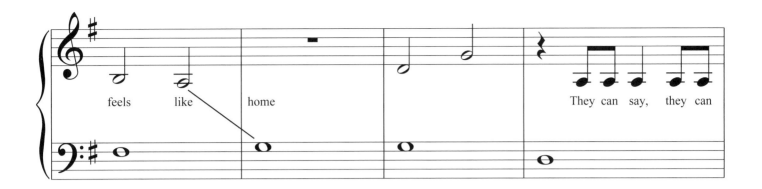

feels like home

They can say, they can

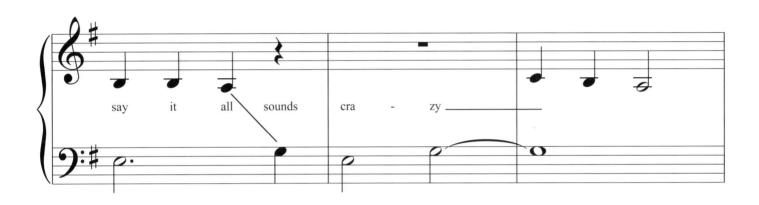

say it all sounds cra - zy

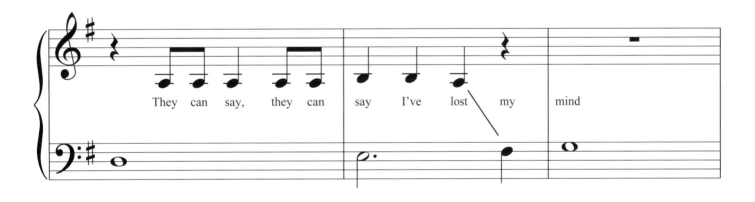

They can say, they can say I've lost my mind

I don't care, I don't care, so call me

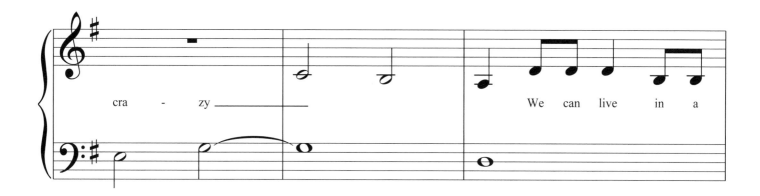

cra - zy _____ We can live in a

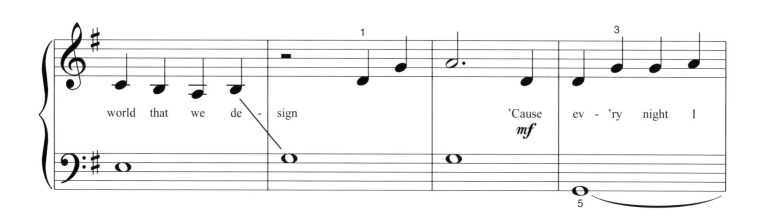

world that we de - sign 'Cause ev - 'ry night I

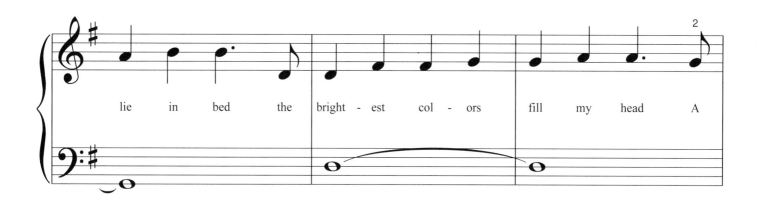

lie in bed the bright - est col - ors fill my head A

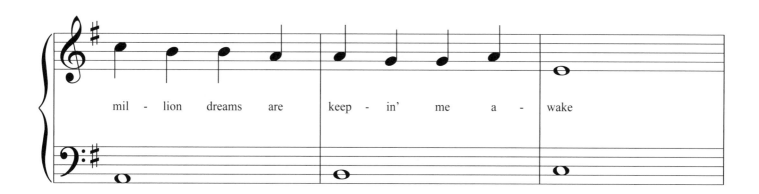

mil - lion dreams are keep - in' me a - wake

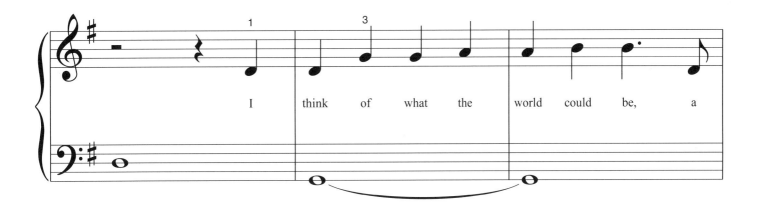

I think of what the world could be, a

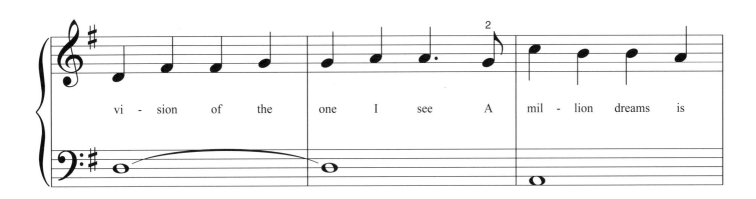

vi - sion of the one I see A mil - lion dreams is

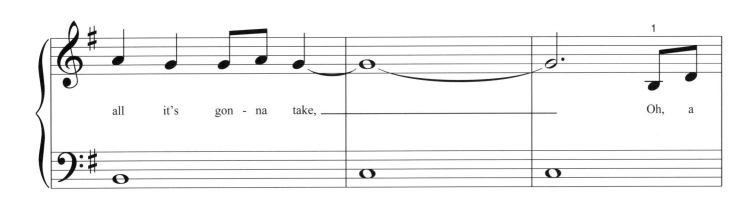

all it's gon - na take, _____ Oh, a

mil - lion dreams for the world we're gon - na make _____

YOUR SONG
from the Motion Picture ROCKETMAN

Words and Music by ELTON JOHN
and BERNIE TAUPIN

Easy Rock

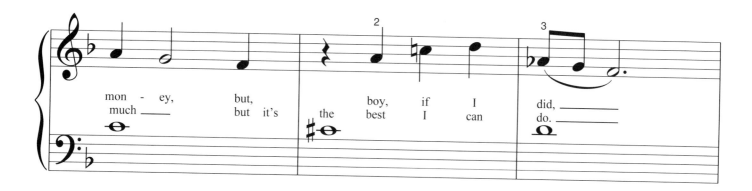

I'd buy a big house where
My gift is my song

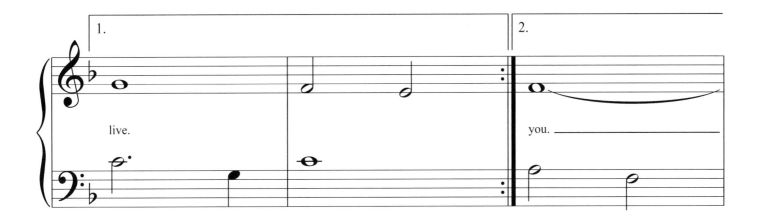

1.
live.

2.
you. _____

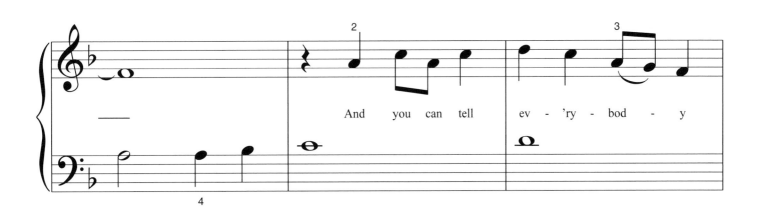

_____

And you can tell ev - 'ry - bod - y

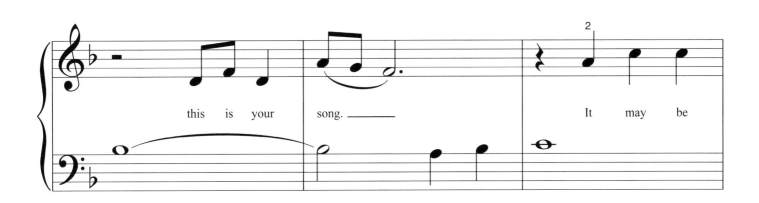

this is your song. _____

It may be

quite _____ sim - ple, but now that it's done, _____

I hope you don't mind, I hope you don't mind

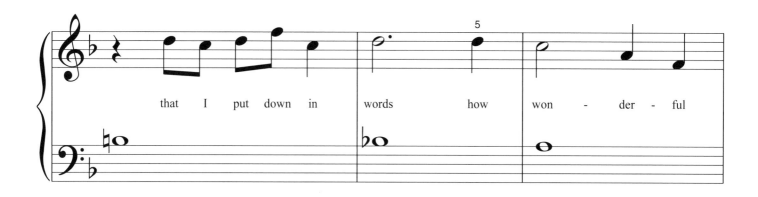

that I put down in words how won - der - ful

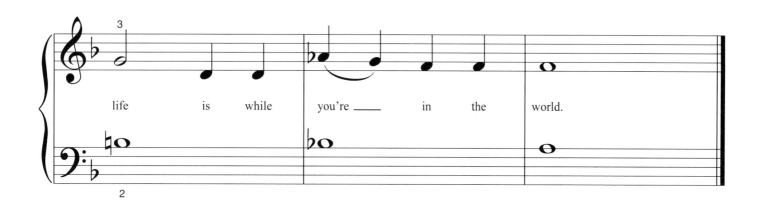

life is while you're _____ in the world.

SHALLOW

from A STAR IS BORN

Words and Music by STEFANI GERMANOTTA,
MARK RONSON, ANDREW WYATT
and ANTHONY ROSSOMANDO

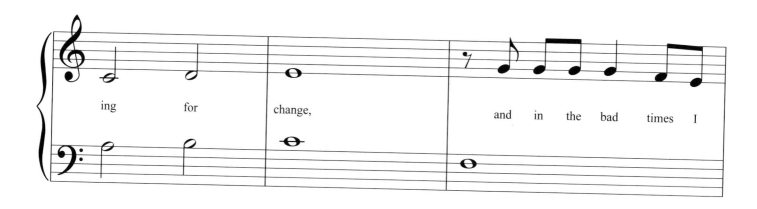

ing   for   change,   and   in   the   bad   times   I

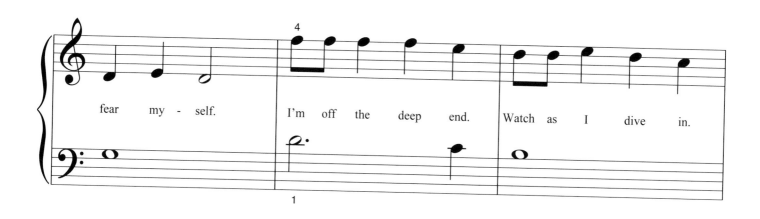

fear   my - self.   I'm   off   the   deep   end.   Watch   as   I   dive   in.

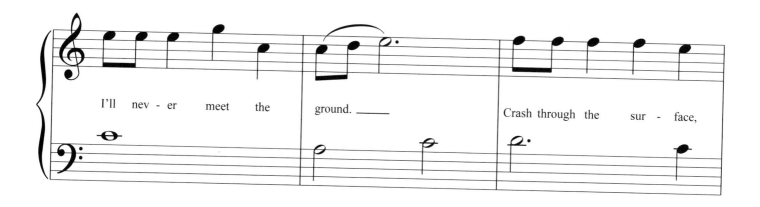

I'll   nev - er   meet   the   ground. _____   Crash through the   sur - face,

where   they   can't   hurt   us.   We're   far   from   the   shal   -   low

now. _____

In the shal, al, shal, - al - low, _____

in the shal, shal, - al, - al, - al - low.

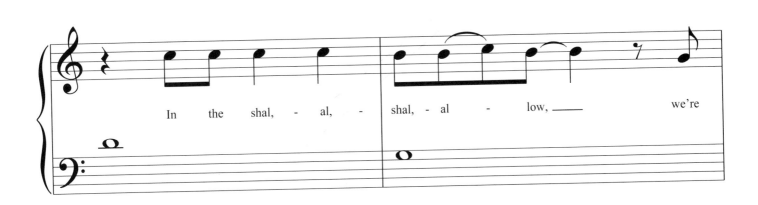

In the shal, - al, - shal, - al - low, _____ we're

far from the shal - low now.

WON'T YOU BE MY NEIGHBOR?

(It's a Beautiful Day in the Neighborhood)
from A BEAUTIFUL DAY IN THE NEIGHBORHOOD

Words and Music by
FRED ROGERS

It's a beau-ti-ful day in this neigh-bor-hood, a
neigh-bor-ly day in this beau-ty-wood, a

beau-ti-ful day for a neigh-bor. Would you be mine? Could you
neigh-bor-ly day for a beau-ty. Would you be mine? Could you

1.
be mine? It's a

2.
be mine? I have

al-ways want-ed to have a neigh-bor just like you! I've

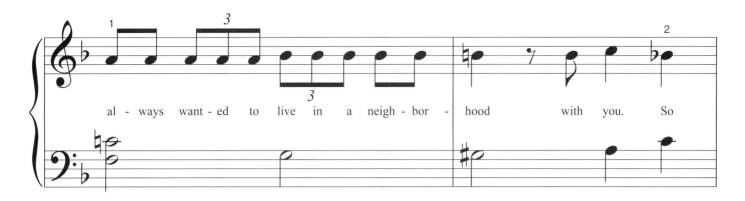

al - ways want - ed to live in a neigh - bor - hood with you. So

let's make the most of this beau - ti - ful day, since we're to - geth - er we might as well say,

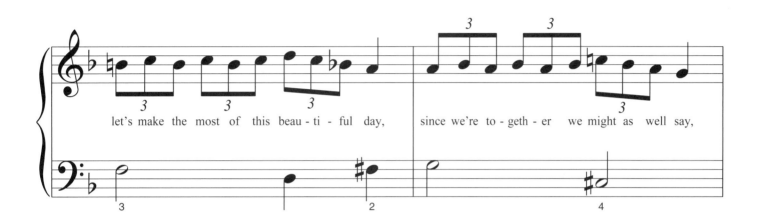

would you be mine? Could you be mine? Won't you be my neigh - bor?

Slower

Won't you please, won't you please? Please won't you be my neigh - bor?

YESTERDAY
from the Motion Picture YESTERDAY

Words and Music by JOHN LENNON
and PAUL McCARTNEY

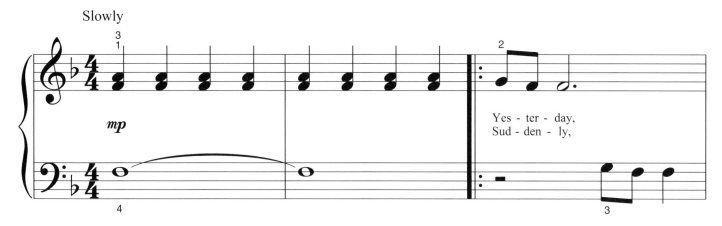

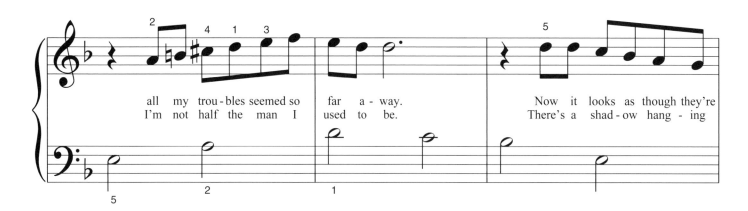

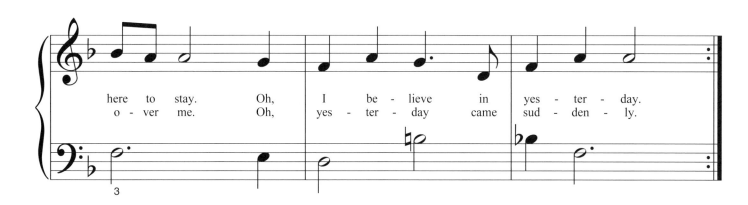

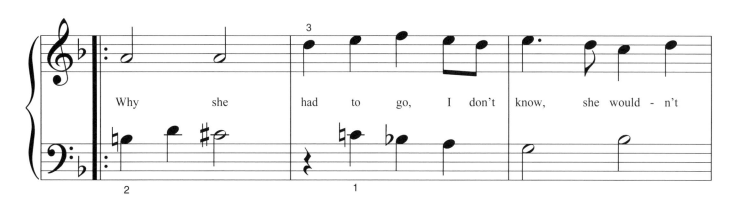

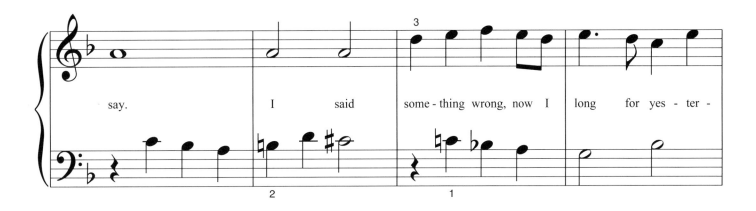

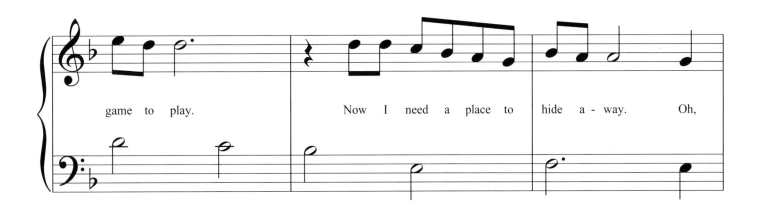

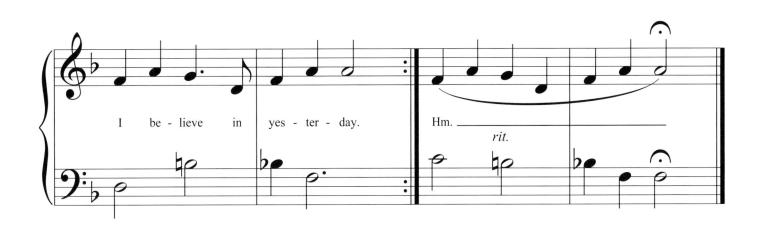

ZERO
from RALPH BREAKS THE INTERNET

Words and Music by DAN REYNOLDS,
WAYNE SERMON, BEN McKEE,
DANIEL PLATZMAN and JOHN HILL

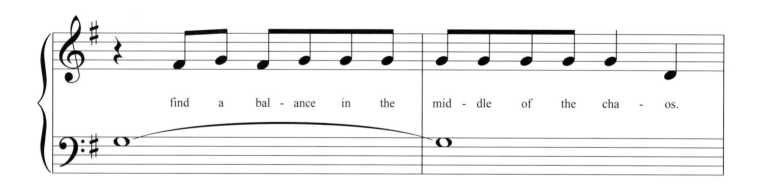

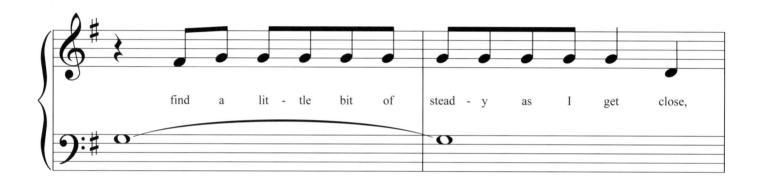

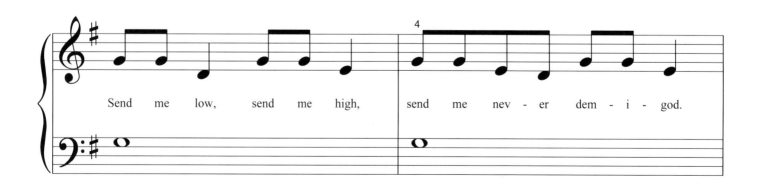

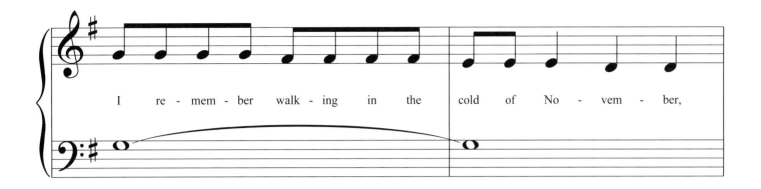

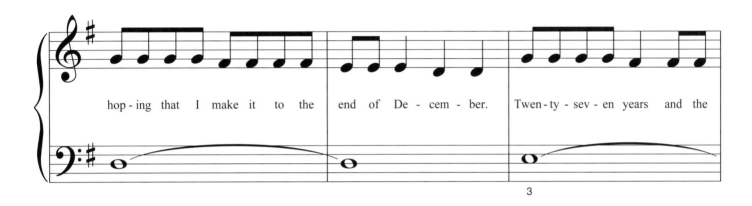

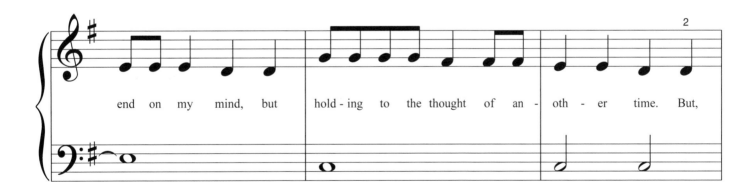

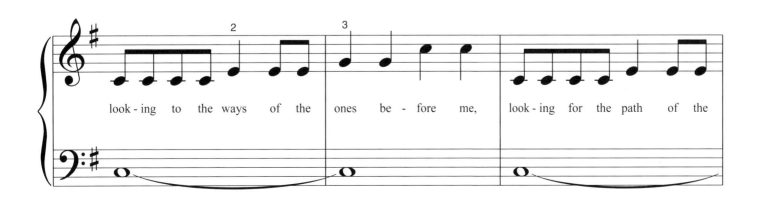

young and lone - ly. I don't wan-na hear a - bout what to do. ____

I don't wan - na do it just to do it for you.

Hel - lo, hel - lo. Let me tell you what it's like to be a

ze - ro, ze - ro. Let me show you what it's like to { al - ways
                                                       { nev - er

feel, _____ feel _____ like I'm emp - ty and there's noth - ing real - ly
feel, _____ feel _____ like I'm good e - nough for an - y - thing that's

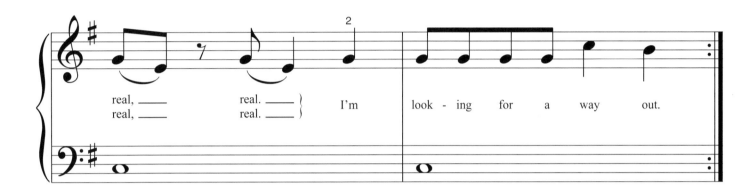

real, _____ real. _____ I'm look - ing for a way out.
real, _____ real. _____

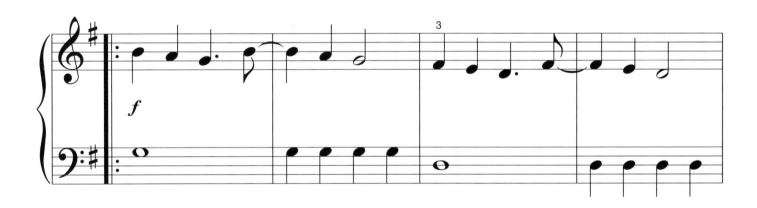

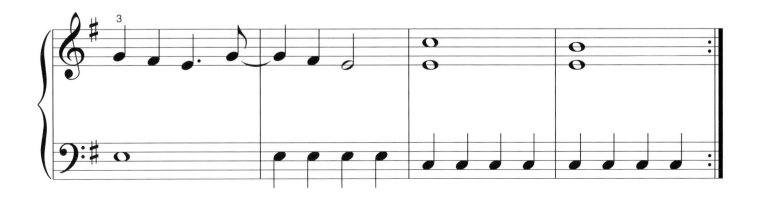

BEGINNING PIANO SOLO

Hal Leonard Beginning Piano Solos are created for students in the first and second years of study. These arrangements include a simple presentation of melody and harmony for a first "solo" experience. See www.halleonard.com for complete song lists.

00153652 **The Charlie Brown Collection™** $10.99

00316058 **First Book of Disney Solos** $12.99

00311065 **Jazz Standards** $9.95

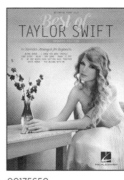

00103239 **The Phantom of the Opera** $12.99

00175650 **Best of Taylor Swift** ... $12.99

00156395 **Adele** $12.99

00311063 **Classical Favorites** $8.99

00130375 **Frozen** $12.99

00118420 **Best of Carole King** ... $10.99

00175142 **Pop Hits** $10.99

00119401 **Tangled** $10.99

00306568 **The Beatles** $12.99

00316082 **Contemporary Disney Solos** $12.99

00311799 **Gospel Hymn Favorites** $8.99

00103351 **Les Misérables** $12.99

00311271 **Praise & Worship Favorites** $9.95

00110390 **10 Fun Favorites** $9.99

00307153 **Songs of the Beatles** $9.99

00311431 **Disney Classics** $10.99

00311064 **Greatest Pop Hits** $9.99

00319465 **The Lion King** $12.99

00316037 **The Sound of Music** ... $10.99

00109365 **Wicked** $10.99

00279152 **Cartoon Favorites** $9.99

00264691 **Disney Hits** $10.99

00319418 **It's a Beautiful Day with Mr. Rogers** $8.99

00110402 **The Most Beautiful Songs Ever** $14.99

00110287 **Star Wars** .. $12.99

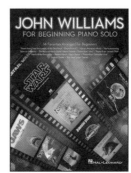

00194545 **John Williams** $10.99

HAL•LEONARD
www.halleonard.com

Prices, contents and availability are subject to change without notice. Disney characters and artwork TM & © 2019 Disney